MAKING PICTURES
and
PATTERNS

Written and illustrated by

HOWARD MELL & ERIC FISHER

SCHOFIELD & SIMS LTD · HUDDERSFIELD

0 7217 4504 0

First Printed 1969
Reprinted 1971
Reprinted 1974

Printed in Great Britain by
W. S. Cowell Ltd at the Butter Market, Ipswich

Contents

A Word of Advice

You will find that you can enjoy making the things in this book much more if you remember some simple rules:

Before you begin: always cover your desk with newspaper. Put out the things you need.

When you are working: do not let things get too messy.

When you have finished: clean the things you have used and put them away. Put scraps in the wastepaper basket.

Keep things tidy – including yourself!

1. *Using Crayons*

Do you like this picture of some sheep?
Tony drew it when he was six.
You can see that, in places, he has pressed hard when he drew
and made a nice thick layer of wax crayon.

When he had finished, he took a soft cloth or a paper handkerchief
(either will do) and polished his picture.
It shone like a well-polished shoe.

Have you tried polishing a picture, I wonder?
Why not try it to see what happens?

When you are using crayons don't be afraid to use the *side* of the crayon as well as the point. To do this, you may have to take off the paper round the crayon, if that is the sort of crayon you have.

Have you some scissors or a knife? Try cutting little bits out of the side of the crayon. The drawings show you what I mean. If you haven't got scissors or a knife, try using a finger nail.

What happens when you draw with the side of your crayon now? Can you see that it makes lines and spaces like the ones in the picture? Try making patterns in this way.

You do not have to press hard all the time. Sometimes crayoning looks nice when it is thin.

6

Look at Jim's picture of a cat. He drew it with crayons — black, orange, yellow and grey. Some of his colours were put over the other colours.

When he had finished his cat, Jim thought it would be a good idea to put in a rug. Can you see it? Can you think how he did it? He mixed some thick red powder paint (it was a red rug). Then he took a big, soft brush and brushed his paint right across the paper, over his drawing of the cat. He was afraid his cat would disappear under the red paint. But it didn't. Why not?

Have you found out that it's because wax and water don't mix? The red paint would not stay on the paper where the wax crayon was. Can you see the little spots of red in the cat's coat? That is where there were little spots of paper with no wax crayon on. The red paint stayed there. Do you think it makes the cat's coat sparkle?

Crayon Etching

Here is another kind of picture to make with crayons.

You will need :

Smooth, but not glossy, paper or card. (Exercise or writing paper will do. Old Christmas or birthday cards are good.) Crayons of all colours – some light, some dark.

Something to scratch the crayon with – a big nail, a paper clip, an empty ballpoint pen (anything which has a point but is not too sharp).

Put down a thick layer of light coloured crayon on your paper or card. Red, yellow, or green will do.

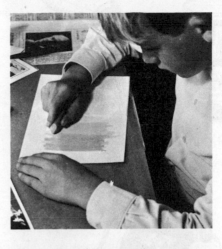

White can be used if you have it. Cover all the card or make patches as in the pictures opposite. Use different colours. Make sure you get a good, thick layer of crayon.

Now cover the crayoning you have just done with a layer of black crayon. Try to get it really black.

Put plenty on. If you find you are not getting a thick, black coating, try another crayon. The one you have used may be too hard or too sharp.

Some people try rubbing chalk on the first colour to help the black to stick.

Here is another way of getting a good black layer of colour. Mix some black powder or poster paint thickly in a jar. Then put in some soap or a little washing up liquid.

You can rub a paint brush on a cake of soap or squirt a little washing up liquid into the paint. Stir the mixture. With a paint brush, cover the crayoning with this black mixture.

When your black layer is finished (it doesn't matter if it is crayon or paint mixture) you are ready to scratch your pattern or picture. Scratch away the black layer to show the yellow or other colour underneath.

The pictures on this page show some of the things done in this way. See what you can do. Try out different ideas.

Using several layers of crayon

If you wish, you can put several different colours on top of one another. You can put three or even more. The picture shows a pattern done like this. It has yellow, blue, red and black layers. The scratching made these colours show at different places. It is a lovely piece of work. Can you do one?

If you wish, instead of putting colours on top of each other, you can put them side by side and then cover them with black. Why not try it?

Crayoning on top of a painting

If you look at this picture, you can see that some of the buildings in it are not finished. It was done in paint and coloured inks. Then, on part of it, Jim has used crayons to put in windows and other things.

2. Chalk and Crayon Transfers

Here is a way of making magic pictures with crayons. I call them transfer pictures because the colour is *transferred* or moved from one piece of paper to another.

You will need:

Some newspaper to cover the desk or table.

Some sheets of paper with a fairly rough surface, like sugar paper, the pasting side of wallpaper or card from a cornflake packet.

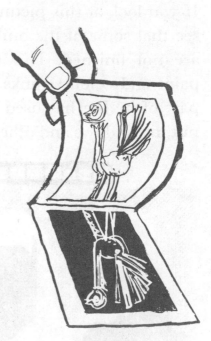

Some thin, smooth paper like typing paper.
Chalks. Wax crayons of various colours.
A ballpoint pen or hard pencil.

On the rough paper make rectangles of chalk as the drawing shows. Use the side of the chalk. Press on and put plenty of chalk on the paper.

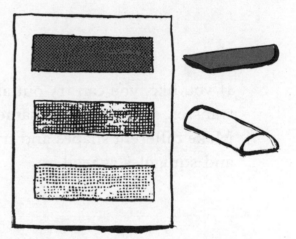

Now cover the chalk with a layer of crayon. Put plenty of crayon on. Rub one way, then the other to make sure you get a really thick layer of crayon. Use a different colour of crayon for each patch of chalk.

When you have finished, you will have several differently coloured patches – one yellow, one blue, and so on. Now you are ready to do transfer drawings.

Next, put a sheet of thin paper —
exercise paper or typing paper —
down on the colour on one of your
transfer sheets. With your ballpoint or pencil, draw a shape and fill
it in. Lift off your thin paper and
look at the other side. What has
happened? You should find the
shape you have made *transferred* to
the thin paper.

If you like, you can try out all your
transfer sheets in the same way.
Make different shapes and try lines
and squiggles as well.

Do you like the way the colour has
been transferred? Can you see that
it looks different from ordinary
crayoning? The texture, that is the
surface or *feel* of the crayon, is
different. It isn't shiny and sharp
like your usual crayoning. How can
you describe it? I call it crumbly and
soft.

Now go ahead and make coloured pictures and patterns. You can work in two ways. Either you can draw with your paper on one transfer sheet all the time. This will make all your picture or pattern appear in one colour.

Or you can move your drawing paper from one transfer sheet to another. Then your work will be in several colours.

Perhaps you will make a face yellow, the hair red, the coat green and so on. Different parts of your pattern can be done in different colours.

Try mixing the colours by drawing on the same place over more than one colour. What happens? I have seen some lovely soft mixed colours made in this way.

There are some patterns Jim made on this page.

3. *Making Rubbings*

On this page you can see some rubbings. Have you ever tried making rubbings? They are quickly done.

You will need:
Crayons or cobbler's heelball (ask your teacher about this).
Some thin, strong paper – typing paper or exercise book paper will do. If you use exercise book paper, make sure it is not glossy.

You will also need something to make rubbings from. What have you got? Have you anything in the room which you can use? There may be coins, leaves, book covers or even a wood floor. Is there something outside to try? What about tree bark or stones? What else is there? Try them.

To get a good rubbing, put your thin paper over the thing you want to rub. Hold it so that it doesn't move. The picture shows you how. To make sure, get someone to hold the paper or pin it or Sellotape it down if you can. Now rub the paper with your crayon. What happens as you rub? You should see a pattern begin to appear on your paper.

Look at these pictures. They were made by making sheets of rubbings. Then they were cut up and used to make sea, planks of the boat, sails, and so on. If you want to make pictures like this, you will need paper, paste and scissors.

Make some rubbings. Cut pieces
out as you want them and paste
them on a sheet of paper to make a
picture. Use different parts of your
rubbings for different things in
your picture. In this picture here,
I have used a rubbing of hardboard
for grass. The tree is part of a
rubbing of a floor board or fence.

Do you see how to do it? You can
make very good pictures with lots
of different textures in them.

If you like making pictures and
patterns in this way, try different
ideas. Could you make a picture
using this sort of rubbing *and* cut-
out pieces? Are you going to try?

4. *All Kinds of Collage*

This picture shows one sort of collage.
It is made from pieces of coloured paper cut from magazines.
Can you see that the mouth is a picture of sausages and the hat is
a helping of Christmas pudding?

Collage is a word we have borrowed from the French. It means sticking things down, or what we make when we stick things down, usually with paste or glue.

There are a lot of different ways of making collages. You can try them — they can be very exciting to do. You can make pictures and patterns in this way.

You can make pictures like this. Have you some old magazines with coloured pictures and advertisements in them? Look through them and see what you can find to make a picture.

You will need :
   Old magazines.
   Paste.   Brush.
   Scissors.   A sheet of paper.

Have you decided what to do? Perhaps there is a shape in a magazine which you like.

Why not use it to make a start on your picture? It could be something to make a body, head or a hat. See what you can find.

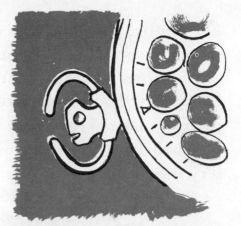

The picture in the middle shows a flower. But it was made from a picture of a fried egg. The drawings show what happened. So you see that you can change the shape of the pictures you find – if you wish.

Cut the pieces out and paste them on your sheet of paper. Try to find plenty of interesting colours and pieces you can cut out and use. What are you making?

Do you like this lion? His eyes are pieces of apricot and his mane was cut from an advertisement for to-bacco. His body is a picture of a piece of material (tweed). I am sure you will have ideas of your own. Try them out.

Making patterns

If you want, you can make patterns in this way. Look at the pattern here. Jim made it. He cut out his pieces and started his pattern in the middle. Then he worked outwards, pasting on the pieces he liked. Can you see what some of these pieces are? I can see fruit and other things.

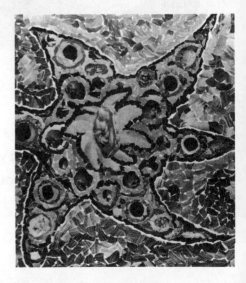

The pattern here is different. Have you made patterns like this?

If you have a big sheet of paper, you could make a very big pattern. Why not work with friends and make it together? You can make your patterns much faster like this. You will each have ideas which you can use.

Are you going to try it? Talk about it with your teacher.

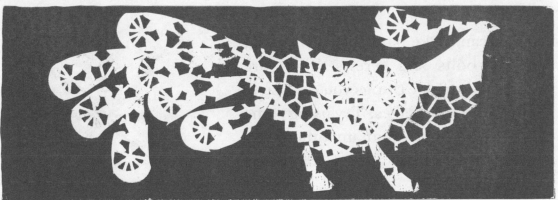

Using doyleys

Do you know what doyleys are? Can you find out? They are very cheap and you can cut them into pieces to make pictures and patterns.

This bird looks very fine. It was made by cutting pieces of doyley and pasting them down. What can *you* make?

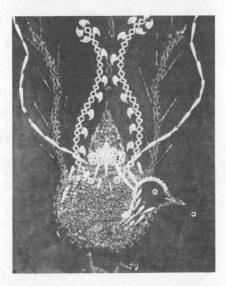

If you want, you need not work only with doyleys. Why not use them with bits of magazine? See what sort of collage you can make. How good can you make it?

String, nuts, bolts and screws

You can make patterns with string, nuts, bolts and screws. They are just a few more things you can use to make good collages. Try using some or all of them – and any others you can find. There are lots of things you can use.

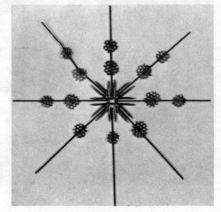

Look at the pattern here. It has nails, screws, nuts and bolts and pieces of wire. What else is there?

I hope this makes *you* want to try this sort of collage. You will need glue instead of paste to make sure that your pieces stick to the paper or card. See what you can do.

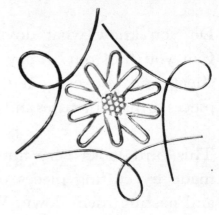

The two collages here are made from string. Look at the bottom one. What is the string glued to?

It isn't paper or card, is it? I think it looks good. It makes the pattern look different. It is an onion bag, begged from the greengrocer.

So you see, you need not fasten your collage to paper or card. I have seen a piece of sack, corrugated card, wallpaper, and other things used for the background.

Have you got something, or can you find something, to fasten your pieces to? Of course you can use card if you wish. The pattern on the right was glued to card.

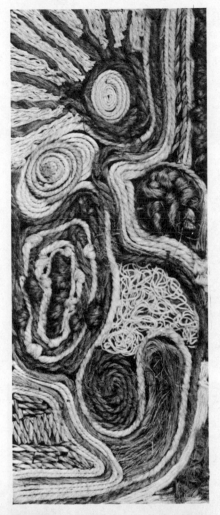

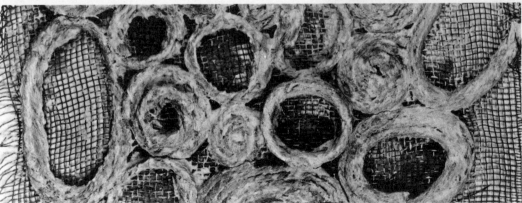

Corrugated card, chocolate trays, toffee papers

Corrugated card, chocolate trays and toffee papers are some more things used in collages made by my children. The one in the photograph at the top of the page has all these things – and others – in it.

There are many other things you can use for collages. Feathers, milk bottle caps, straw, wood shavings, paper fasteners, lollipop sticks. These are just a few things you can use. Try your ideas out. See what happens when you use a new idea.

Look at the picture on the left. It is a pattern made from corrugated card. But instead of the card being fastened down flat, it has been cut in strips of different widths and glued on its edge. Can you see?

Collect odds and ends and use them as you like. Go ahead and make pictures and patterns. Make your collages as good as you can. Keep on trying out different things and different ideas. You will be able to make some very good collages.

This strange animal was made from corrugated card with a milk bottle top for an eye, pieces of egg box for legs and what else?

Patterns and pictures made in this way give you a lot of chances to try out new things. Because unusual things can be used, they can be very exciting to do.

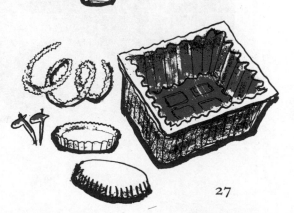

Paper pushing

Here is a way of putting ridges and other shapes into paper to make patterns and pictures.
The picture here and the mask on page 29 were made in this way.

You will need :

    Paper or card.

    Paste and paste brush.

    Coloured tissue paper (Fruit wrappers would do).

Put plenty of paste on your paper or card. Make it really thick. Now tear a piece of tissue paper and put it down on the paste. Push the paper with your fingers as the drawing shows.

What sort of wrinkles and ridges can you make in the tissue paper? Can you make a pattern? Push the paper in different ways. Try making different ridges and valleys in the paper. How many different ones can you make?

The lively clown was made in this way. Can you make pictures too? You can push the paper into lots of little wrinkles or leave some of it flat. This makes a change.

See how interesting you can make your pictures and patterns by changing the surface of the tissue paper; that is, you change the *texture* of the paper.

Try pasting the tissue first, before you put it on the card. Lift it up gently by the corners. Lay it, paste side down, on the pasted card. The two pasted surfaces come together. Now push the paper into different shapes. Do you like this way better?

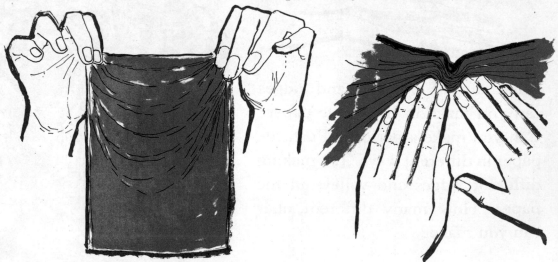

30

Of course, you can put this sort of work together with other things to make your work even better. All the ways of making collages we have talked about can be used with tissue paper. Use anything you think will look good. So do not be afraid of using nails and paper, sacking and string, feathers and wallpaper pieces, and so on.

This jolly old lady has raffia hair, a tissue paper face, newspaper beads, and a wallpaper blouse. I like her very much. Do you?

What are *you* going to make? See what you can do. There are many ways of using paper pushed like this.

Collage with cloth and other materials

A lot of very nice pictures and patterns can be made from bits of wool, cloth and other materials.

Try something simple to start with, like this little dog. He is made from odd pieces of coloured cloth. His head is white and black, his collar is blue and his body is nearly white.

You will need :
  A piece of paper or card. Scissors.
  Paste and a paste brush.
  Bits of cloth and other fabric.

Decide what you are going to make. Cut out the pieces you need and paste them on the paper or card. Add any little pieces you like to make your picture or pattern as good as you can. Try an idea of your own. What can you think of?

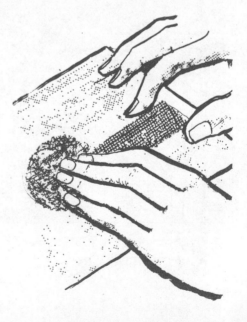

When you have tried something simple, you will see how easy it is to make colourful pictures and patterns. Try using a lot more things in your work.

The pattern at the top of the page has bits of cloth, wool, cotton, nylon stocking and a few odds and ends like paper fasteners and milk bottle tops. Can you see some of them?

Some parts of the pattern are made more attractive by putting pieces of coloured net in different places. Some of the pieces overlap one another to give another effect.

You will find it a help to try how things look before you paste them down. As you work, put the pieces down on your paper or card. How do they look?

Would it be better if you moved some of the pieces? Which do you think is the best position for them?

Would it be better if one piece or more overlapped?

Does it look better if you add some other shapes or change one or more of those you have used?

Would a piece of net improve it?

When you have tried out different arrangements and got one which you like, stick the pieces down. Then try placing more pieces to see whether you can improve what you have got.

I have seen pictures and patterns made like this in shops and art galleries. Some people I know sell them for a lot of money. They can make very good decorations for walls. The one below was done by a girl.

Stitching patterns

This picture was made by a girl aged 10. It is made with pieces of material, but instead of sticking the pieces down, she *stitched* them onto a piece of hessian.

Do you like stitching? Some of my boys do it and enjoy it. How surprised the girls are! Some of the stitching can be part of the pattern, like that in the picture on page 36.

You can't really tell from this drawing, but in a pattern like this
different sorts of thread would be
used. Some are thin, some are thick
and they are of different colours.
Then some have different textures;
there is fluffy wool and smooth
cotton and even a bit of thin string!

Do you think that these stitches
would help to make the picture
better? Do you think the colours
and the textures would add something to the picture?

Why not try this idea and see what
you can do? If you want, you can
stick some parts down and then
stitch your patterns on them. I
think you could make a very nice
pattern or picture.

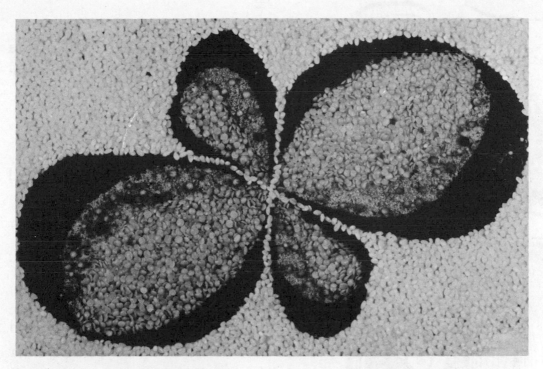

Collages from the kitchen

I am sure that you can see now that you can use almost anything for making collages. If you haven't thought of it yet, here is an idea which my children use. They enjoy it very much.

Can you guess what was used in these pictures? All the materials came from the kitchen. There are peas, beans, lentils, tea, egg shells, sago, rice and other things. And there are a lot of other things which can be used.

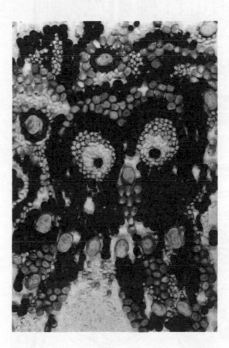

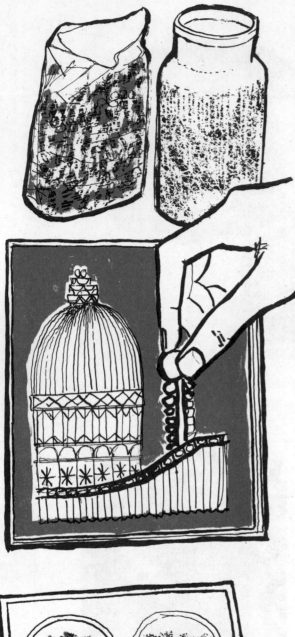

What can you make? What have you got which can be used to make your picture or pattern?

You will need :
A box lid (though a piece of card or thick paper will do).
Polyfilla or putty. (Plasticine or dough can be used.)
Things from the kitchen.

Both Polyfilla and putty are good to use. If you use putty, put a layer in the box lid or on the card. Pat it smooth. If you have Polyfilla, put a layer of it in the lid. Do not mix Pollyfilla thinly, it needs to hold the pieces you push into it.

Have you decided what you are going to make? A picture of what? A pattern? What sort of pattern?

Take what you like from your kitchen things and push them into the putty or Pollyfilla. Try using several different things to make the picture or the pattern better to look at. See how good you can make it.

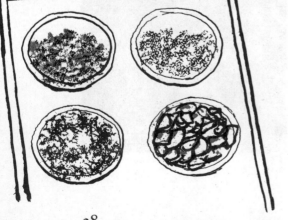

Can you cover all the lid or card?
What are you making? If you use
Polyfilla, it will not be long before
it dries and hardens, so try to work
quickly. If your layer *does* dry,
brush a *little* water on the part you
haven't covered. Then add a little
more Polyfilla. This will give you
more time to finish your work.

You may need to make shapes by
using a number of the same thing.
For example, the background for
the cat on page 40 was made of tea
leaves. Do not be afraid of using
shapes *and* lines in your work.

You need not use only things from the kitchen. If you want to try using them, why not see how other things look when they are used? Buttons, beads, straw, silver paper — these are just a few ideas. I am sure you will have ideas of your own. What are you going to try?

Can you see why I suggest using a lid? It helps to stop things rolling off onto the floor. And it makes a sort of frame for your work when it is finished.

All my children love making pictures and patterns in this way. It is just another sort of collage, isn't it?

So now we can leave collages. There must be hundreds of ways of making them and thousands of different ones to be made.

Try as many ideas as you can. I wish I could see what you have made.

5. *Patterns You Can Look Through*

Do you like patterns like these on this page? They are made from pieces of coloured paper or cellophane. If they are put on a window, the light comes through and makes the colours glow.

The top one looks like a church window. It looks like stained glass. Do you know what stained glass is? Can you find out about it? Perhaps you can find some pictures of stained glass. Some of it is hundreds of years old and is very beautiful.

You can make the pattern first and then fasten it to the window or you can put your piece of paper straight onto the glass as you work. Discuss this with your teacher.

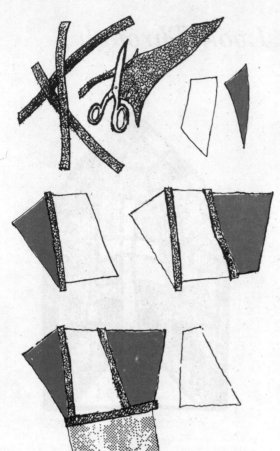

To make a "stained glass" pattern, cut black paper into strips about one centimetre wide. Cut the shapes you want from the tissue paper and stick them together with the black strips. These can be cut as long as you want them. The drawings show how it is done. Keep adding pieces until the pattern is as big as you want it.

If you work straight on to the glass of your windows, do not use a lot of paste. You need very little, just a touch of paste here and there to make the tissue paper stick.

Hanging up your patterns

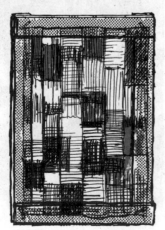

There is no need to put this sort of work against a window if you do not want to. If you wish, you can make a frame of cardboard strips and fasten your pattern to it.

Notice that you can join several frames together if you wish.

Another way of making a frame for your pattern: cut a hole or holes in a cardboard box or box lid.

Using materials you can see through can make other things look more interesting. Here are two. Both the animal and the bird were made from thin cardboard. Holes of different shapes were cut and covered with tissue paper or cellophane. As they twist against the light, the colours glow. Can you make something like this? I expect you have a lot of ideas to discuss.

These look very well hanging in a room. If you can make them twist round and round, they can look better still. If they can be hung where they catch the light, then so much the better.

6. Painting

I expect you have painted since you were very small. Do you enjoy it?

Probably, you have painted with powder colour. There are other sorts of paint which you may have used. What are they?

What sort of brushes have you used? I hope you have bristle brushes and soft brushes. Have you small *and* big brushes? Whatever sort of brushes you have, have you found out what sort of marks they make?

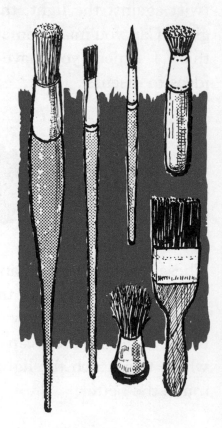

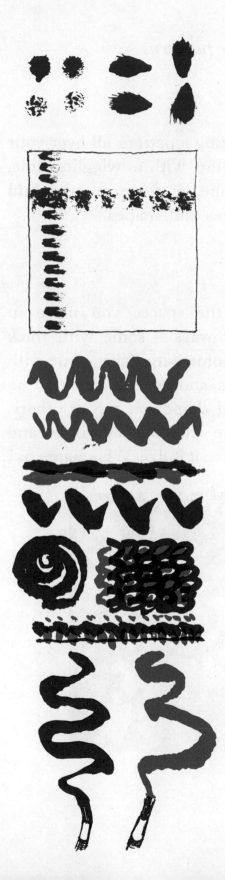

Try mixing some paint and then see what marks you can put on your paper. Try pressing the end and then the side of the brush on the paper. What is the difference? Do a line of each mark right down or across the paper. The drawings show you what I mean.

Try making thick lines and thin lines by pressing lightly or heavily on the brush as you paint. What happens when you *dab* the brush on the paper? If you have different brushes, do they make different marks?

Have you tried making marks with both hands at once? Take a brush in each hand. Now use both brushes – paint down from top to bottom.

Making patterns

There are some of the marks I have mentioned on this page. They could be used when you make patterns. Here are some patterns to try.

All-over patterns

Try making a pattern all over your paper. Start with a wiggling line, or a shape, or your initials. Add more lines and shapes.

Fill in the spaces you make in different ways – some with thick colour, some with dabs, some with squiggles and so on. Try putting lines and shapes on top of others. Try some when the paint is wet and some when it is dry. What happens?

Go on until your paper is covered with colours. Do you like your pattern? Can you make better ones?

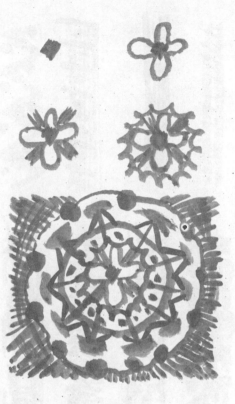

Another way of working is to start in the middle of your paper and work outwards. Make a shape in the middle of your paper. Add lines and shapes until you reach the edges of the paper. The pictures show you what I mean. Try it and see what happens.

This sort of pattern can be made by working together with friends. Make a mark in the middle of the paper and then you all work round the mark, making a pattern together.

Stripe patterns

Try making patterns with stripes. Stripes can be more than just one straight stroke of colour. There are many ways of making them. You can start with a line. Then add more lines and shapes to make the stripe more interesting.

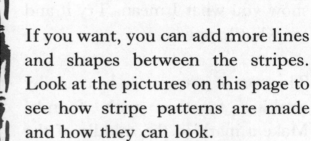

If you want, you can add more lines and shapes between the stripes. Look at the pictures on this page to see how stripe patterns are made and how they can look.

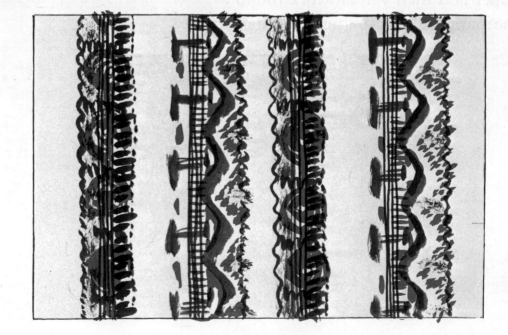

Now try to make a pattern of your own. Try to make your stripes really good. See how different your patterns can look when you use different stripes like those in the picture on page 48.

Try putting your stripes in a circle, like spokes in a bicycle wheel.

Repeat patterns

These are the patterns you make when you *repeat* the same shape over the paper – like the one here.

Jim painted a round shape and then added lines and other marks. He made his pattern easier to do by folding his paper before he began to paint.

The drawings on this page show how to fold the paper.

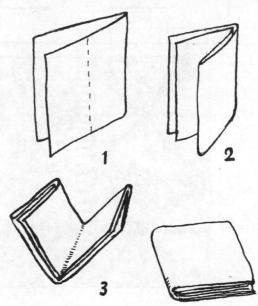

When it is opened out, the marks of the folds leave rectangular shapes on the paper. These help you to see where to place your marks. The drawings here show you what I mean.

Jim also painted the pattern at the bottom of the page. Can you see that the pieces of pattern do not make a straight line? Each piece is half way down the next. Jim did it by folding the paper as before. Then he drew lines across the middle of four of the spaces. When he did his pattern, he placed marks as in the pictures here.

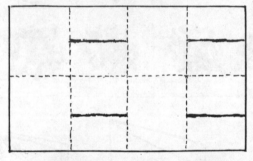

Can you make a pattern like this? It is easy when you see how to do it.

Instead of painting a starting shape, you can cut a template or a stencil from paper. Then you can make repeat patterns from them. You can find all about this in Printing page 24.

That book tells you about many ways of making prints. Why not make patterns by printing part and painting others? Anything which makes your pattern more interesting is worth trying. Have you realised, for example, that you could make patterns with paint and collage? Why not try? Try other ways of making patterns, you will find a lot of different ways, I'm sure.

See what you can do.

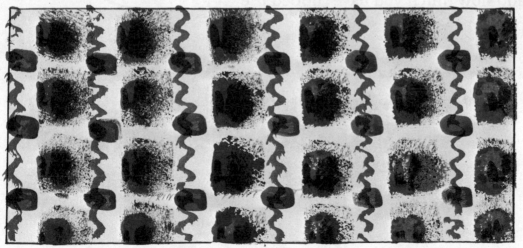

Starting with blobs

Here is another way of starting a pattern. Put a shape near the middle of your paper with rather wet paint. Put on plenty of paint. You can make your shape long or short. Please yourself, but do not make it very small.

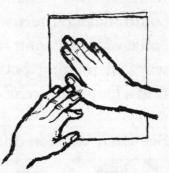

While the paint is still wet, fold your paper in two. Put it down on your table and rub your hand over the paper where the blob is. Rub it hard.

Now open your paper again. What has happened? This will depend on how much paint you have put on and how much you have rubbed the paper.

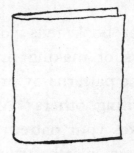

What can you add to the new shape you have made to make it a good pattern?

Here are two patterns made in this way. Notice that one of them is done on paper which has been cut to make it long and narrow. Can you try a shape of paper like this?

If you want, you can paint your paper all over first. Then put a blob of a different colour in the middle, while your paint is still wet. Now fold the paper as you did before.

Sometimes, these blobs make you think of faces and figures. You may like to change your blobs into faces or go on and make a picture. See what you can do.

Mixing paint with other things

There are a lot of ways of making your paint look different when it dries. It is worth trying them because they can add interest to your painting. Try some of these: sand, Gloy or Marvin Medium, paste, sawdust.

Mix in one of these with your paint. See what happens. Then try mixing more than one – say Gloy, sawdust and paint. What is it like when it dries?

If you try mixing things like this in your paint, you can make your patterns and pictures more interesting to look at. You have made different surfaces and a change of surface can be a help in a painting.

So make experiments with mixing and then see if you can use them in your work.

Paint with collage

There are many ways of painting. Do not forget that you can use collage and paint together. Try this way.

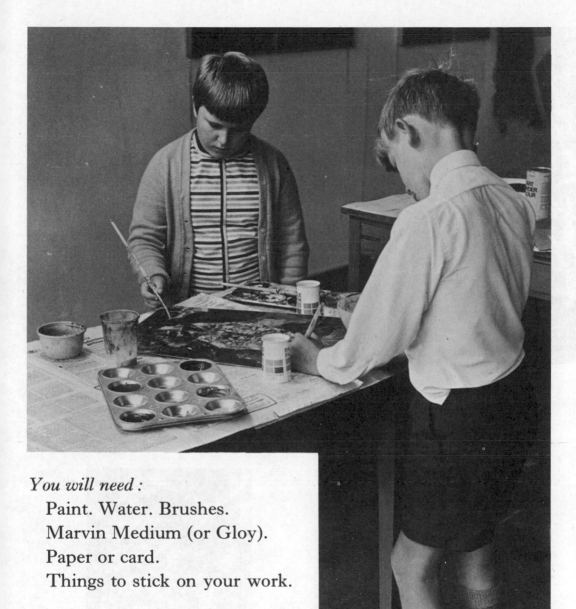

You will need :
Paint. Water. Brushes.
Marvin Medium (or Gloy).
Paper or card.
Things to stick on your work.

Mix your paint with some Marvin Medium or Gloy. Keep your brushes in water when you are not using them – this will keep the brushes from becoming hard.

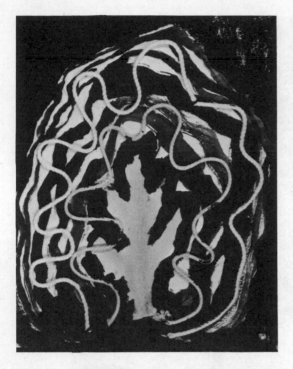

When you have painted and while the paint is still wet, push into it any pieces which you want to add.

The picture here was inspired by a cabbage cut in two. It has bits of string pushed into the paint. Can you see them? Perhaps you have something you can look at and paint and then add some collage?

When you want to make a picture, don't automatically think you have to *paint* the objects you want to show. Sometimes your pictures can turn out better if you mix your methods.

56

There are two small paintings shown at the bottom of page 56. Look closely at them. They have pieces of newspaper, toffee paper, string, corrugated card, and even pieces from a pencil sharpener.

Why not try this sort of painting? If you like, you can work like this when you are doing other sorts of painting – when you paint people, or when you imagine the things you paint. So remember these ideas later.

I like pushing paper (we did this on page 28) and then painting on top of it.

The picture at the top of the page shows one which Jim did. He soaked some tissue paper in paste, put it on a sheet of card and then pushed it with his fingers to make a pattern. When the paper was dry, he painted it in different colours.

This, then, is just another way of painting and I hope you can see what you can do.

Using inks

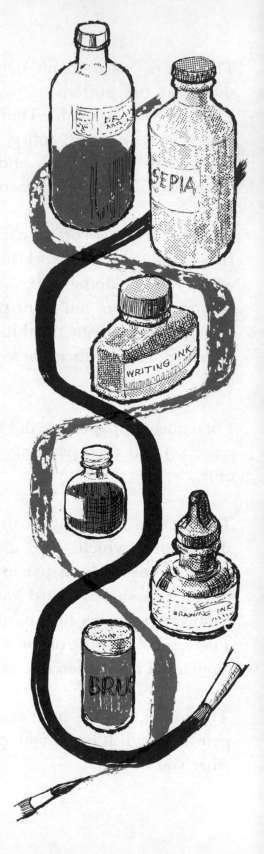

Of course, you needn't always use paint in your painting. Try using inks as well as paint. They give a different finish to your work. Some of the colours are very lovely. You can mix them with water and make them so thin that you can see through the colour.

Try inks by themselves and try them together with paint. If you ask your teacher, there may be some Brusho colours you can use. These are very cheap and make very bright colour.

Most of the other things I mention in this book can be done with ink. Try to remember this.

There are other things which can be used in your picture and pattern making. See what you have available and try it. I have seen a very good picture which had some shoe polish in it!

Pictures and patterns without brushes

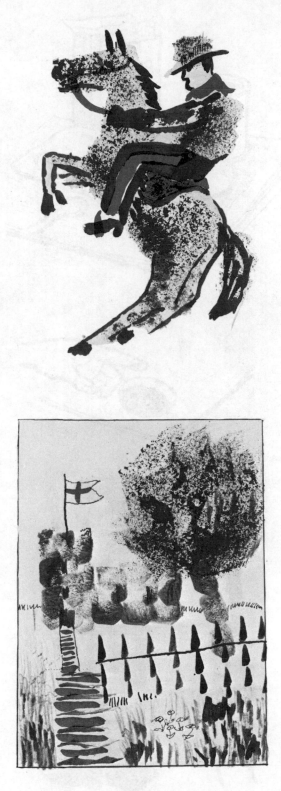

You can make pictures and patterns without using brushes. If you look at "Printing" – you will see what I mean. In that book, I talk about using sponges, string, rubbers and other things. They can be used for patterns and pictures. They can be used with paint and inks.

The picture here is partly painted and partly printed. The picture at the bottom was done with a small piece of sponge and rubber. It is very good.

So try making your pictures without using brushes, or using brushes for only a part and some other things which make marks for the rest. You can get different effects from those you get when you use only brushes. See what you can do. What do you think of the results? I hope you will go on trying different ways of making pictures and patterns.

Finger painting

This is another way of working without brushes. You may have painted with your fingers when you were younger. But try it again. Now that you are older, you can do much better work.

You will need :
    Paste. Paint. Water. Paper.
    Mixing tin or plate. Spoon.

If your teacher has mixed some starch with soap flakes use this instead of the paste – it can be better. If the colours have not been mixed for you, put some of the paste or starch mixture into your mixing tin. Then stir in some paint.

Put in plenty of powder colour and mix it in well. When you have put in enough paint and mixed it well with the spoon, you are ready to start.

Pick up some of the mixture on one finger and put it on the paper. You can put it on thinly or thickly, just as you wish. Try both. Make a pattern or picture, using several colours. Mix the colours together on the paper if you want.

In your patterns or pictures, you can make marks with the end of a brush, a piece of card or an old comb. If you wish, you can cover the paper with thick colour and then make your pattern with fingers, card, or what you like.

This way of painting can be fun. It can be used with paper pushing, collage and other things. The picture here gives you an example. I hope you try this and see what you think of the results. They can be very good.

You can take a print from your finger painting. Press on some thin paper while your work is wet. Lift it off. What have you got?

Painting from imagination

All the painting in this book so far has been done from imagination. You have not copied anything. You have put down what was in your mind or made marks to see what happened.

Have you looked in a fire and imagined that the flames were people dancing? Have you watched clouds and imagined that they were animals or space craft? Do you imagine people and places when you read a story or a poem? I expect you do.

It is fun to make pictures or patterns when you have read a story or a poem, or written one yourself. The picture on page 64 was painted from a story.

Try to imagine pictures and patterns as you listen, read or write. Then make your painting.

Of course, you can imagine things for your picture *and* put in things which you have seen. Perhaps you have read a story about boats or are learning about fishing.

If you can, look at some books and find out what different boats look like. Perhaps it is a story about Vikings. What sort of boats did they use? What sort of weapons?

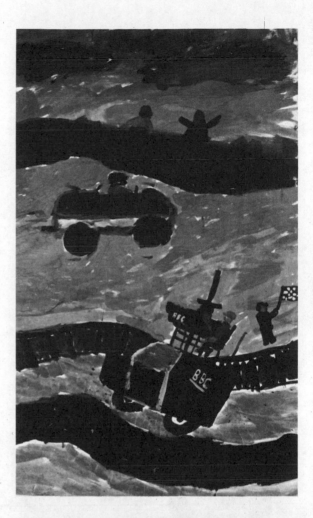

Talk about what you are going to do. It may give you more ideas. Then your painting may be much better.

Painting does not mean making pictures and nothing else. I expect you have painted models and some of the things you have made from paper.

Have you painted masks, belts or head-dresses (like Indians' for example)?

There are a great many pieces you can make for use in plays and story acting. These may be things to wear or carry. What about some small pieces of scenery? All these can help to make your work in drama much more exciting. Talk about this and see what you can do together.

Painting can make a lot of your class work more enjoyable. It can help you to understand what you are studying.

Painting what you see

Have you tried painting a picture of yourself or a friend? To paint yourself you will need a mirror. Keep looking in the mirror as you paint.

Ask a friend to stand or sit in front of you. Perhaps your friend could be reading a book or holding something, such as a toy or a pet. Make a good, big painting to fill the paper. If you are taking a long time, do not forget to let your friend have a rest.

Do not hurry with your painting. Go on steadily and look hard to see that you know exactly what your friend looks like. Are you going to paint the background? What is your friend sitting on or standing on?

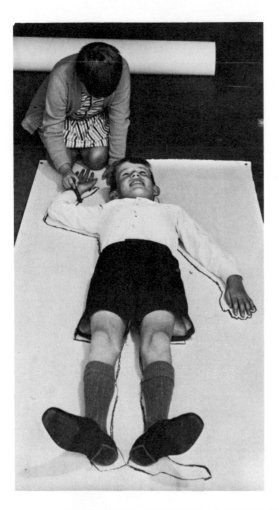

Another way of painting someone is to use several sheets of paper. This can be newspaper. Fasten the sheets together to make one big sheet. Make it a little bigger than the person you are going to paint. Perhaps you have a roll of wallpaper? Why not use a large piece of it?

Put the sheet on the floor and let your friend lie down on it. With a piece of chalk or crayon, draw carefully round your friend. Alison is doing this in the picture.

Are you going to change places when you have made another big sheet of paper? Then your friend can draw you.

When you have made the shape of your friend, paint inside it to finish it. Or you may have a piece of material, say an old shirt, which you can stick on to make a body. Then something to make a tie.

If the person in your picture is reading a newspaper, perhaps you would like to stick a real newspaper in his hands. Perhaps you can join with other friends and paint it together.

A collection of these figures would look very good on the wall.

In my room, there are a lot of things to paint. Here are some of the things I have: Feathers, shells, lamps, stuffed birds, pebbles and stones, models, bark from trees, pots, bottles, pieces of cloth, an old boot, and many more. All these are used in paintings.

Then there are things I borrow or buy such as fruit, vegetables, fish, dishes, a bicycle, a drum, and so on.

You may have some of these things, or others, in your room. You may have brought them yourself. My children bring leaves, tadpoles, twigs, flowers and nuts.

What have you got which you would like to paint? Try painting them separately or put them together to make a pleasing group. Perhaps you have helped your teacher make a group.

Are you going to paint what you can see behind your objects? What else are you going to put in? Do you know where all your objects came from?

Have you a pet you can paint? Can you have it to look at while you paint? Perhaps someone can hold it. Or perhaps you can go and look at birds or animals and then come back to paint them. This would be painting from memory, wouldn't it? Talk about this with your teacher.

Here are two paintings of animals. One was painted with the animal in the room. The other was painted from memory. Which is which, do you think?

Remember that your pictures do not always have to be on ordinary rectangles of paper. I like to paint long thin pictures like this.

This shape of paper made Jim think of a cellist.

Painting from memory

I hope you can paint other things you have seen. Why not paint something you have seen on a visit or near your home? Have you been to the fire station and then painted a fire engine and the firemen? Have you painted what you saw on your holiday? Or the trees you saw in the park or in the country?

Keep your eyes open when you make a visit. Notice how things look. Then talk about them and paint them. Was the sky *really* blue? Or was it another colour? Did you notice what all the other things looked like? Were you able to hold or feel some of the things?

There are thousands of pictures to be painted. Remember that you can make pictures with many different things and not only paint. Try out your ideas and keep on trying to make better and better pictures. On this page are some paintings done by my children.

7. *Drawing*

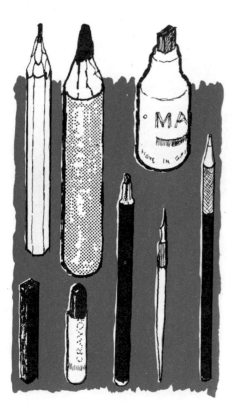

When you draw, what do you draw with? A pencil? A pen? I wonder what sort of pencils and pens you use. I hope you can try soft and hard pencils and thick and thin ones. And what about pens? Have you tried ballpoint pens and felt pens?

If you have them, or can get them, I think it would be fun to use charcoal (or charcoal pencil), chalk,

conté crayon (pronounce this "con-tay" crayon – it is a French crayon). See what sort of marks you can make with these. I have put some of them on this page. See what you can do. Try making patterns with zig-zags, loops, squiggles and other marks.

How does your drawing look if you draw on dark paper with white and other coloured chalks and crayons? Don't forget you can draw with the long side of your paper upright, as well as across.

I am sure you have drawn on your blotting paper sometimes. Try drawing with pen and ink on a clean piece of blotting paper. The ink dries straight away and you get a lovely soft effect.

All the things I have mentioned for you to paint can be drawn. You can draw people or objects you see, or things from memory or imagination. And you can draw on top of paintings and patterns. The picture here was done in this way. Can you see the parts which have been drawn? Have you tried this? Why not do it now? Talk about it with your teacher.

It is a good idea, now and then, to work with a group of friends. My children enjoy doing this. They made the picture at the top of the next page.

First of all, they talked about what they wanted to do. Each one then drew a person or an animal and cut it out. Then they put a large piece of paper on a table and stood round it. They painted a background and pasted their drawings on it. They worked very hard until the picture was complete. Do you like it? They liked it so much that they made three more and fastened them on a wall.

The next picture was made by another group of children. They had been reading and talking about a port, so they decided to make a picture of a port. Each of them agreed to make a part of the picture. When they had finished, each part was pasted to a large piece of paper to make one picture.

Would you like to make pictures like these? Have you formed a group? Now you will have to decide what you are going to do. What is the subject? What are you going to use? Will it be paint, crayons, collage, or what? Perhaps it will be more than one of these? Are some parts going to be printed? Will someone need to paint a background?

You will have to discuss this with your teacher. As well as the things I have mentioned, you will need: scissors, paste, brushes and a large piece of paper so that you can all work round it or stick all your work on it. You can make a large piece of paper by sticking smaller pieces together. If you have nothing else, try using newspaper.

Here is another idea. Each one in the group draws or paints a picture. Then the pictures are pasted together in one long line. There is a picture made like this at the bottom of the next page.

Can you see that the road joins together? It is just as though one person had painted it. You see, the children decided how big the road was going to be. Then, when they had finished, all the pieces of road could be joined together. If you do work together, I hope you will remember to do this.

Are you going to try? Yes? Then don't forget to decide what you are going to do and how big things are going to be. I hope you will try many more of this sort of picture.

Remember that you can make patterns together. Remember, too, that you can paint, draw, print, push paper, use rubbings, or anything you want in the same picture or pattern.

So we come to the end of this book. You should try each way of making a picture or pattern more than once – the more times the better.

Your later efforts will probably be better than your earlier ones as you get more practice. Go back in the book and try again some of the things you have done earlier.

I do hope you will keep on making pictures and patterns. I am sure you will enjoy doing them. Good Luck!

Index